# CLARINET
# For
# Beginners

T0080161

## AVRAHM GALPER
### Revised Edition

**BOOK I — ELEMENTARY**
**BOOK II — INTERMEDIATE**
**SCALES AND ARPEGGIOS**

## BOOSEY & HAWKES

AN IMAGEM COMPANY

DISTRIBUTED BY

## HAL•LEONARD®
CORPORATION

7777 W. BLUEMOUND RD. P.O. BOX 13819 MILWAUKEE, WI 53213

Dedicated to the memories of Tzvi Tzipine and Simeon Bellison

## PREFACE

CLARINET FOR BEGINNERS is based on the Chalumeau or the low register. It has been my experience that spending more time in the low register will be of greater benefit to the player later on.

There is a scientific reason for this: most wind instruments require more air pressure when going into the higher registers. The clarinet is different. It requires less air pressure when one goes from low to high. However, in order to do this effectively, one must build up a certain amount of air pressure in the low register first.

Beginners generally play on soft reeds. As they advance they should 'graduate' to harder ones, which necessitate more blowing pressure but will also facilitate the transition from the Chalumeau to the higher registers.

I use the 'long tone' approach: instead of actually sustaining long tones (which are, in fact, very beneficial) I have substituted slurred material. The pieces and exercises should be played slowly and sustained at first to get the benefit of the 'long tones'. Pupils can then 'tongue' the exercises, after having played them slurred first.

Teachers can start the pupils on G, E or C, starting at the appropriate note or line on page 4.

**AVRAHM GALPER**

## EMBOUCHURE

The embouchure is the lip and mouth formation around the mouthpiece when playing. A good basic embouchure is formed when pronouncing the vowel "oo" and smiling at the same time. Another good basic embouchure is formed when whistling (and trying to smile at the same time). Using this embouchure, one should lower the jaw a bit to make room for the mouthpiece in the mouth. The lower lip should be turned in slightly over the lower teeth to form a cushion under the reed. The upper teeth should rest lightly on the mouthpiece about 3/8th of an inch (10mm) from its tip and the upper lip should form a seal around the mouthpiece to prevent air from escaping. The clarinet should be kept at a close angle to the body (about 35 degrees).

## INITIATING THE SOUND

With the mouthpiece and reed in the mouth and the embouchure formed:
1) LIGHTLY touch the reed with the forward part of the tongue.
2) BLOW (there should be no sound since the tongue prevents the reed from vibrating).
3) While still blowing, quickly but gently, pull the tongue away from the reed and the sound should start.

## PRACTICE

The pupil should endeavour to practise EVERY DAY rather than skip a few days and then attempt to make up for lost time. It is better to practise less time but WELL rather than practise a lot without organization.

The motto should be: practising PERFECTLY makes perfect.

© Copyright 1970 by Boosey & Hawkes (Canada) Ltd.
Revised Edition © Copyright 1980 by Boosey & Hawkes (Canada) Ltd.
Boosey & Hawkes, Inc., Sole Agent.
Copyright for all countries. All rights reserved.

Printed in U.S.A.

## FINGER POSITION

The fingers should be curved slightly as if you were holding a tennis ball with the finger tips. The fingers should not be lifted too high and should be kept over their respective tone holes and keys.

## SOUND

One should practise slowly and produce the best sound possible. Until a good embouchure and tone are formed, it is best to play mezzo-forte (medium loud). Once there is control, one should also play the pieces and exercises softly. Pupils should listen to good clarinet players and recordings in order to acquire a 'conception' of a good clarinet sound and imitate it to the best of their ability.

## THROAT NOTES (The 'break')

Throat notes require special attention: in order to have a smooth transition between registers, it is better to play these notes slightly louder. Since pupils play them softly, it is better to get into the habit of playing throat notes with more sound. Ease the sound when crossing the 'break' upwards so that the transition is not forced.

## FINGERINGS

New fingerings are presented with a chart and picture of their own. The pupils should learn these carefully and memorize the various alternatives. Knowledge of different fingerings will be useful in future playing.

The following are explanations of some of the **signs** used in this book:

a) TOGETHER ⌐_____⌐ , play the notes above (or below) this sign, TOGETHER. Use the fingering indicated.
b) Although there are other notes between the first B and C, play the first B and C, TOGETHER without removing the fingers for the intermediate notes.
c) LEAVE ON ⌐_____ In the transition C to B, leave the C key depressed while playing B.
d) This sign is a combination of two LEAVE ON's.

## BREATHING (while practising)

Where there are no natural breathing places, such as a rest or a long note followed by shorter notes, I suggest the following: When a breath is needed:

1) Come to a stop on the first note of a bar (or the first of a group of notes)
2) Hold the note for two beats (while still counting)
3) Take a breath, start on the next beat with the note you stopped on, and continue.

4

Start the sound with the tongue. Once started, keep it steady throughout the bar. Do not stop the sound with the tongue.

$\frac{4}{4}$ means that there are four beats to a bar. A whole note ○ has four beats.

♪ = *Take a breath*

♩ : is a half note. Two half notes equal one whole note ♩+♩ =○ Each half note has two beats. Start the slur ⌣ with the tongue. All the other notes under the slur are not tongued.

𝄴 is the same as $\frac{4}{4}$ Remember: once started, keep the sound steady.

In a WHOLE note there are four quarter notes. In this FIRST TUNE you will find quarter notes and half notes. Beat one beat for each quarter note, two beats for each half note. Tongue the beginning of each slur.

**FIRST TUNE**

$\frac{2}{4}$ means there are two beats to a bar. 𝄆 is a repeat sign. Any music between such signs is to be repeated. When you need a breath in any of the following mechanisms, take it after finishing the last bar. Repeat each mechanism many times.

## MECHANISMS (Finger exercises)

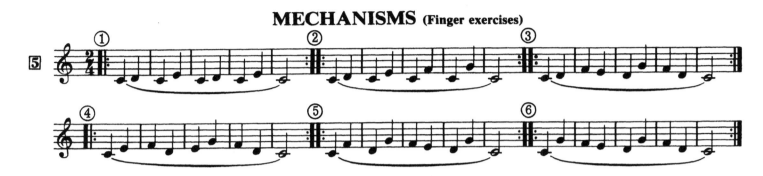

Each time you put down an additional finger to play a lower note, take care that the fingers you already have down do not uncover the holes they are on. If you find it difficult to play the lower notes, most likely you have uncovered one of the upper finger tone holes.

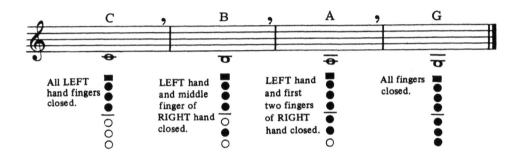

A dot after a note means that the value of the note is increased by half. $\dot{\half} = \half + \quarter$  $\frac{3}{4}$ means that there are three beats to the bar.

## MECHANISMS

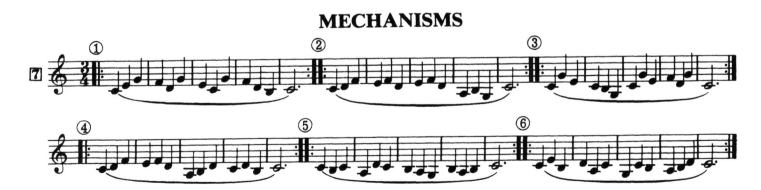

6

## MELODY

### POLLY

**Play this slowly**

### ORANGES AND LEMONS

In music there are rests at which time you do not play (you count, though). In the following line you will find the most common rests. A whole note rest (4 beats) is a small bar under the fourth line. The half note rest (2 beats) is a small bar above the third line. The quarter note rest (1 beat) looks like this:

1 2 3 4    1 2 3 4    1 2 3 4

**Do not breathe at each rest**

### LONG LONG AGO

D.S. al Fine means: Go back to the sign ( 𝄋 ) and play until Fine (end)

*Fine*

*D.S. al Fine*

# CHRISTMAS CAROL

Watch for separate and slurred notes.

An accidental (♯ or ♭) in front of a note will apply to all the same notes in the bar.

# EXERCISE ON B♭

With a very sustained sound

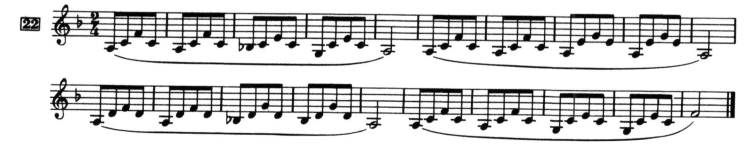

Practise the following exercise slowly, lifting and lowering the fingers gently. Play as smoothly as possible. (Note: B in this exercise is always B♭).

Bb is played by opening up keys 10 and 12. Key 12, known also as the 'speaker' key or 'register' key, is taken with the LEFT hand thumb.

## LONGING

## YANKEE DOODLE

Most of the notes in this tune are articulated ("tongued").

## TIED NOTES

When you see a slur over two notes that are the same, do not tongue the second one but merely add its value to the first note.

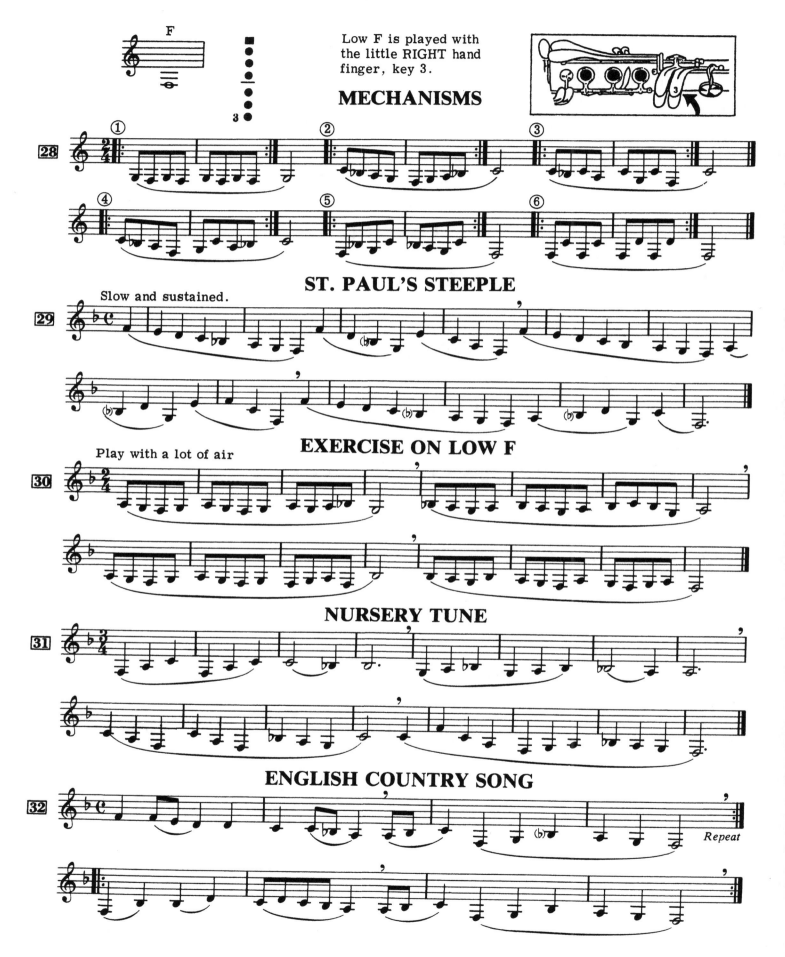

**MECHANISMS**

**ST. PAUL'S STEEPLE**

**EXERCISE ON LOW F**

**NURSERY TUNE**

**ENGLISH COUNTRY SONG**

Low E is played by adding Key 1 to the fingering for low F. Key 1 is played with the little finger of the LEFT hand.

## MECHANISMS

## EXERCISE ON LOW E

*D.C.* means: Da Capo, 'go back to the beginning'. Then play until the ⊕ (Coda) sign, jump to the Coda and play until the end.

⊕ Coda

D.C.

## GOLDEN SLUMBERS

Raise and lower your fingers gently. Play with a smooth sound.

Play F♯ with the first finger of the LEFT hand

# MECHANISMS

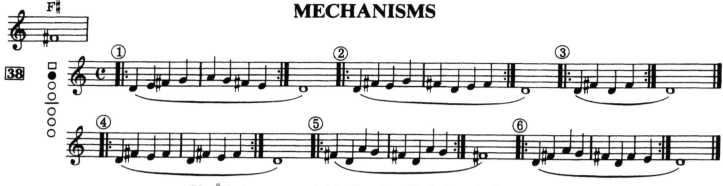

The ♯ that you see right after the Clef sign, indicates that
this piece is in the key of G. Every F will be sharpened.

Most of the notes are tongued

All the notes in this "disguised" piece are articulated. What else is different?

# MECHANISMS

'R' under E♭ means: play E♭ with key 7, RIGHT hand.

# HERE WE GO GATHERING NUTS IN MAY

♮ *(natural)* cancels out any ♯ or ♭

**THE DOTTED QUARTER** ♩. = ♩ + ♪

A dot after a note means that the value of that note is lengthened by half.

These two bars should sound the same.

Count: 1 & 2 & 3 & 4 &

## DOTTED QUARTER STUDY

Count:    1 & 2 & 3 &    1 & 2 & 3 &

## EARLY ONE MORNING

Take care to play the slurs as marked

## THE HURON CAROL

14

The Ab key (key 9) is opened with the side of the second joint of the LEFT hand's forefinger.

## MECHANISMS

## EXERCISE ON Ab

## LULLABY

Slow

## JOHN PEEL

*Two sixteenths* ♬ *equal one eighth* ♪ = ♬

At first play this tune in 4, with each eighth getting one beat. Then play it in two, two beats to a bar.

D.S. al Fine

## THANKSGIVING SONG

## DECK THE HALLS

In mechanism No. 1 keep the LEFT hand little finger on the key all the time. In mechanisms 2 & 3, the LEFT hand little finger and third finger should move together so that there is no intervening note between C♯ and D. In No. 5-practise to get good co-ordination. No. 6-the same as No. 2 & 3

♮ (*natural*) cancels out any ♯ or ♭

The sign %  means that this bar is the same as the preceeding one.

## HOME SWEET HOME

\* G♯ is the same as A♭. See top of page 14.

16

# J'AI DU BON TABAC

Alla Breve: two beats to a bar.

# ORANGES AND LEMONS

'R' under low F♯ means: play F♯ with the RIGHT hand little finger (Key B in picture)

# COVENTRY CAROL

Observe the 'natural' in the last two bars.

Raise and lower your fingers gently. Blow steadily and smoothly.

Play low G♯ with the little finger of the RIGHT hand. (Key 4)

During mechanism No.1 keep the Right hand little finger on key 4 all the time. In No. 2, move the 3rd and little finger of the RIGHT hand together so there is no intervening note between G♯ -A.

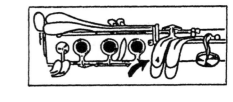

## MECHANISMS

## ENGLISH SONG

Observe the articulated and slurred notes

## SWEDISH SONG

Moderately

## OLE KING COLE

Up until now you have been playing in the Chalumeau ('Shallumo') register of the clarinet. The Chalumeau was an instrument that existed until about 1690 when an instrument maker, Denner, invented the CLARINET by providing a 'Register' key to facilitate the playing of the upper registers. This 'Register' key is the one you know as B♭ (key 12, taken with the thumb of the LEFT hand) Play the low register note for two beats rather firmly, then gently press the 'Register' key and play the upper note softly. Keep the LEFT hand thumb on the tone hole and blow steadily throughout the change. A firm reed will facilitate the register change. Memorize the names of the new notes. These notes are part of the 2nd or 'Clarion' register.

Play the upper notes softer than the lower ones.

First tune in Clarion (upper) register

More clarion notes

Play the lower line in the Chalumeau register first. Then play the Clarion notes above. Think of the names of the new notes as you play them.

## MECHANISMS

Play the upper notes softer than the lower ones.

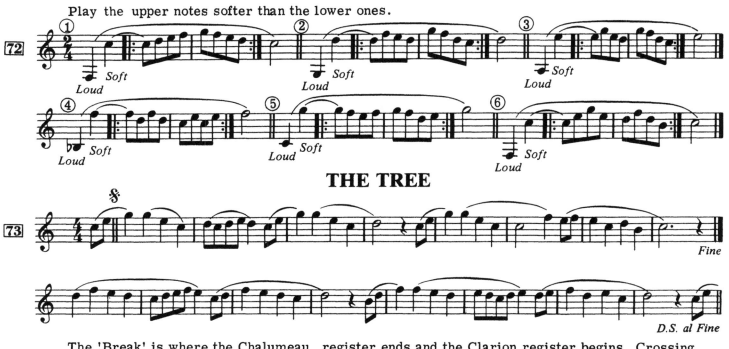

## THE TREE

The 'Break' is where the Chalumeau register ends and the Clarion register begins. Crossing the 'Break' requires careful preparation. In the following mechanisms keep the LEFT hand fingers close to the tone holes. The first finger of the LEFT hand should "roll" over slightly to open the 'A' key while staying close to its tone hole position.

## 'OVER THE BREAK' PREPARATORY MECHANISMS

Second ending: When you reach the repeat sign, go back to the beginning and repeat. When you get to ending 1., skip it and go to ending 2.

When crossing the break downwards (B to A) make sure not to lift the LEFT hand forefinger off the tone hole before opening the 'A' key. Pretend you are playing mechanism No. 4 (above) when crossing the 'Break'. At the same time you may keep the RIGHT hand fingers down plus the little fingers of both hands pressing on their respective keys.

Play the Note A louder

Look up the fingering sign explanations on page 3. Get used to keeping the little finger keys depressed when possible. R: RIGHT. L: LEFT.

**FAREWELL, WINTER**

Play the Notes A and G louder

Low E with the LEFT hand
little finger alone (key 1)

**THE BEE**

'L' under the note B means: play it with the little finger of the LEFT hand alone. Look up other signs on page 3.

**GIRLS AND BOYS COME OUT TO PLAY**

Play A and G louder

# SWEDISH SONG

Do not force the sound upwards over the 'break'.

TRIPLETS. Instead of playing two notes to a quarter you now play a group of three notes. When crossing the 'break' play the break notes a little louder to ensure uniformity between the registers. Look up the sign meanings on page 3.

Break (throat) notes.

Ease the sound over the 'break'.

## 'OVER THE BREAK' STUDY

*D♯ is the same as E♭

The fingering for clarion F♯ is the same as low B♮

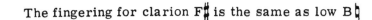

**86**

## MOZART THEME

**87**

Up until now the main bar divisions were quarter notes. In the following $\frac{3}{8}$ and $\frac{6}{8}$ pieces the main divisions are eighth notes.

At first play the following $\frac{3}{8}$ in 3 beats to a bar, then 1 beat to a bar.

**88**

## IRISH SONG

**89**

**Scale & Chord of G Major**

**90**

## MINUET

## LOW E-F♯ TRANSITION

Practise the transition from E-F♯ and F♯-E until it is smooth.

Keep the little fingers 'on' the keys when playing these exercises.

## SING A SONG OF SIXPENCE

## OVER THE HILLS

Alla breve: in two

## SCOTTISH SONG

In each quarter note there are four sixteenths. ♩ = ♫♫

**95**

1 & 2 & 3 & 4 & 1 2 3 4

1 & 2 & 3 & 4 &

## MECHANISMS

**Practise slowly**

**96** ① ② R L

③ ④

*Low F♯ with Left alone*

**97** L

① ②

③ ④ ⑤

*Low E with Right alone*

R means: RIGHT hand little finger

**98** ① ② ③ ④

When low E preceeds or follows low C♯, play the E with the RIGHT hand little finger. Learn the use of either little finger to play low E.

**99**

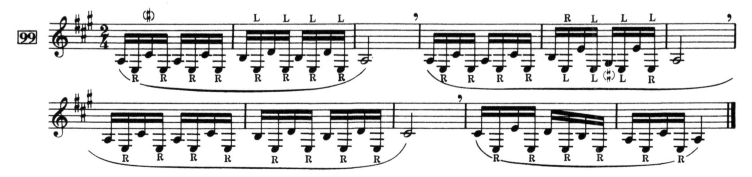

Write in your own fingerings.

When crossing from throat B♭ to the upper register, leave the 'Speaker' key (key 12) open. Make sure you close the LEFT hand thumb hole.

## MECHANISMS

At first four beats to a bar. Each eighth note gets one beat. Then play in two beats to a bar.

**Rondo**

Count   1   &   2   &   1   &   2   &

## DRINK TO ME ONLY WITH THINE EYES

**In a slow 6**

Andante   ⁊ = eighth rest

*Fine*

*D.C. al Fine*

## THE LORELEI

At first in 6, then 2 to a bar.

**Moderato**

1 2 & 3   4   5 6

26

## THE MINSTREL BOY

**Scale of F Major**

**Chord of F**

The HALF notes represent the upper register notes. The lower notes represent the same fingering in the low register (without key 12) Practise slurring from the low notes to the high notes.

You need a good reed for higher notes

When you get to D.C. (Da Capo), go back to the beginning and play until the FINE.

## NOWELL

# BLUE BELLS OF SCOTLAND

**Scale and Chord of C Major**

The 'X' fingering for E♭ is: LEFT hand thumb and first finger of each hand. The mechanism that operates this note should be kept well regulated or else the note will not respond readily. When assembling the clarinet, take care that both parts of the mechanism fit properly. This fingering is sometimes called "Forked" or "One and One". After practising these mechanisms with the 'X' fingering, practise them also with the RIGHT hand fingering, key 7. Although a bit sharp in the low register, the 'X' fingering is useful in certain technical passages.

\* **Low G♭ is the same as F♯**

Low E with the RIGHT hand little finger.

# MECHANISMS

Practise the transition B to C♯ and back so there is no intervening note between them. The little fingers of the hands should be kept'on'the keys when playing these notes

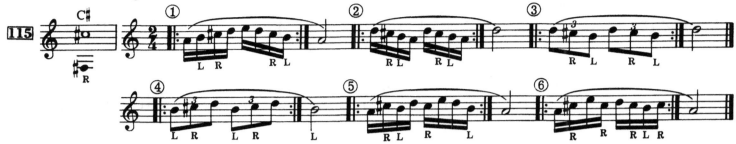

# RIGAUDON

A dance invented by Rigaud, Dancing Master of King Louis XIV.

# MARCH OF THE MEN OF HARLECH

The breath at the end of bar 4 must be taken quickly.

# HOME SWEET HOME

# INDIAN QUEEN

# J'AI DU BON TABAC

# OVER THE HILLS

# MECHANISMS

Play E♭ with the little finger of the RIGHT hand. (key No. 4) See page 17 for low G♯

# EXERCISE ON E♭

C  ( low F )  with the
LEFT  little finger

## MECHANISMS

## THE STEEPLE

## MY SWEETHEART

At first, play in 3. Each eighth note  will get one beat. Then play it one beat to a bar.

## HOME SWEET HOME

*
A♭ is the same as G♯

# ALL THROUGH THE NIGHT

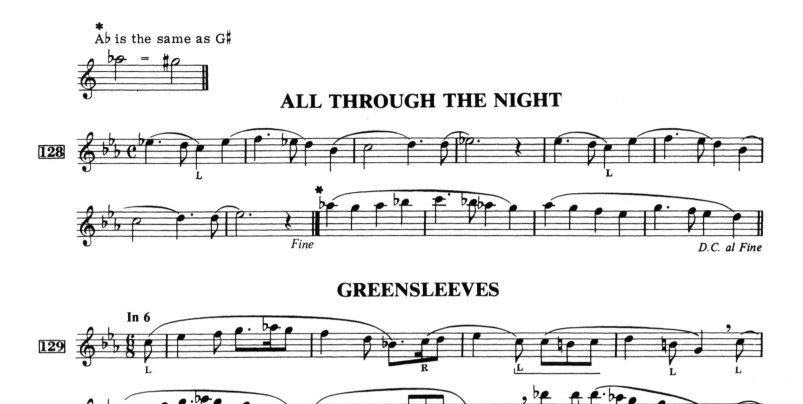

Fine

D.C. al Fine

# GREENSLEEVES

In 6

# MECHANISMS

E♭ with the LEFT hand. 'L' under E♭
means: play it with the third finger
of the LEFT hand (key 7 bis)

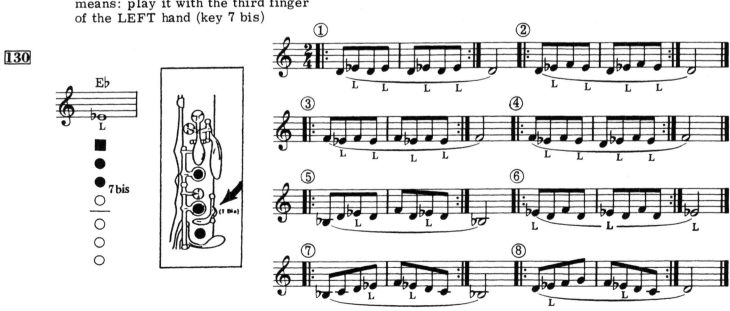

# ETUDE ON E♭

For breathing, look up BREATHING on page 3.

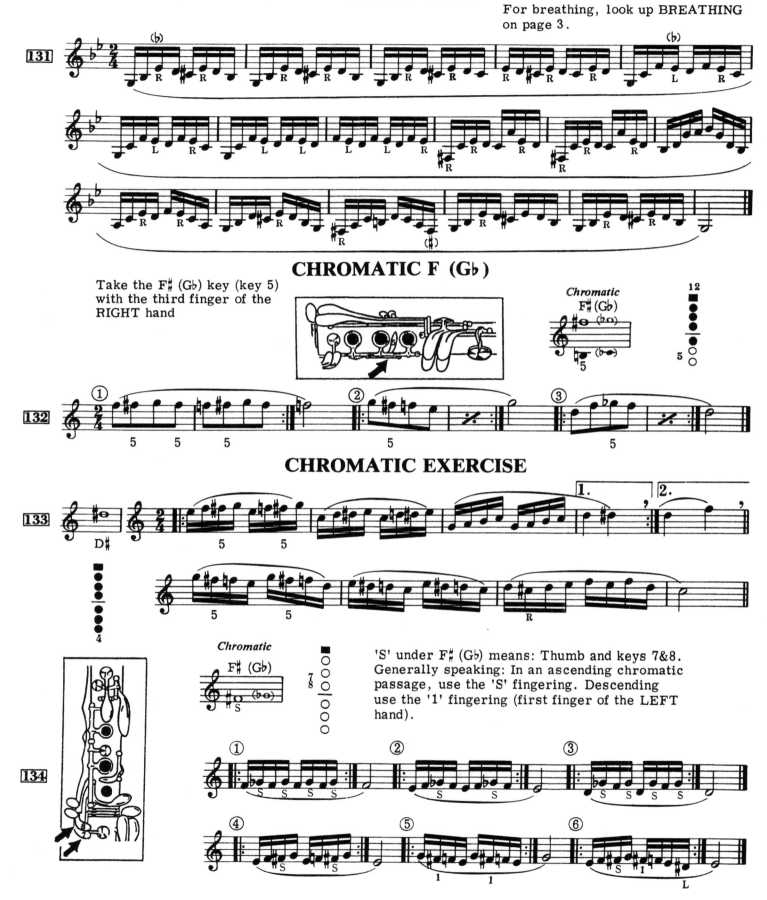

## CHROMATIC F (G♭)

Take the F♯ (G♭) key (key 5) with the third finger of the RIGHT hand

## CHROMATIC EXERCISE

'S' under F♯ (G♭) means: Thumb and keys 7&8. Generally speaking: In an ascending chromatic passage, use the 'S' fingering. Descending use the '1' fingering (first finger of the LEFT hand).

# CHROMATIC EXERCISE

─────── means: Start softly and increase the sound gradually. (Crescendo)
─────── means: Start loudly and decrease the sound gradually. (Diminuendo)

Do not make the CRESCENDO or DIMINUENDO too soon. Make them towards the middle of the bars.

**Slowly**

**Andante (Slow)**

# STACCATO

Staccato means: 'detached' or 'separate'. Up until now you have been starting the sound with the tongue. To play staccato effectively one also stops the sound with the tongue. The procedure is as follows: 1) Lightly touch the reed with the tongue 2) Blow 3) Move the tongue away from the reed – the sound will start 4) Lightly touch the reed and the sound should stop. Touching the reed should be done with the lightest touch and with the front part of the tongue. Play staccato with a lot of air. Generally speaking: the value of staccato notes is halved i;e: a quarter notes becomes an eighth note followed by an eighth rest etc.

### TWINKLE TWINKLE LITTLE STAR

### MIXED SLURS AND STACCATO

### STACCATO ETUDE (Study)

Another staccato exercise may be found in the top line of the first duet on page 36.

Give the 2nd note of each group full value. Play with lots of air.

## THREE STUDIES

Play with lots of air.

Play with lots of air.

# THREE DUETS